OAE 015 Educational Leadership

By: Preparing Teachers In America™

This page is intentionally left blank.

Publication by Preparing Teachers In America Publication Services, a division of Preparing Teachers In America

ISBN-13: 978-1542872966

ISBN-10: 1542872960

This page is intentionally left blank.

Free Online Email Tutoring Services

All preparation guides purchased directly from Preparing Teachers In America includes a free three month email tutoring subscription. Any resale of preparation guides does not qualify for a free email tutoring subscription.

What is Email Tutoring?

Email Tutoring allows buyers to send questions to tutors via email. Buyers can send any questions regarding the exam processes, strategies, content questions, or practice questions.

Preparing Teachers In America reserves the right not to answer questions with or without reason(s).

How to use Email Tutoring?

Buyers need to send an email to onlinepreparationservices@gmail.com requesting email tutoring services. Buyers may be required to confirm the email address used to purchase the preparation guide or additional information prior to using email tutoring. Once email tutoring subscription is confirmed, buyers will be provided an email address to send questions to. The three month period will start the day the subscription is confirmed.

Any misuse of email tutoring services will result in termination of service. Preparing Teachers In America reserves the right to terminate email tutoring subscription at anytime with or without notice.

Comments and Suggestions

All comments and suggestions for improvements for the study guide and email tutoring services need to be sent to onlinepreparationservices@gmail.com.

This page is intentionally left blank.

Table of Content

This page is intentionally left blank.

About the Exam and Study Guide

What is the OAE Educational Leadership Exam?

The OAE Educational Leadership is an exam to test potential individuals' competencies in leadership skills necessary to pursue an educational leadership role in school institutions. The exam is aligned with the updated practices used to ensure effective leadership.

The exam is timed at 225 minutes and consists of 70 select-response questions and four written performance assignments. The questions are based on knowledge obtained in educational leadership programs. The exam contains some questions that may not count toward the score.

What topics are covered on the exam?

The following are some topics covered on the exam:

- ensuring for retention of high performing staff
- developing leaders within the organization
- ensuring proper professional behavior
- recruiting and retaining staff
- inducting new faculty members
- evaluating professional learning
- allocating resources
- using effective assessment procedures
- providing corrective feedback
- developing emerging leaders
- delegating tasks
- assessing teacher-leadership
- supporting sustainable relationships
- enhancing leadership practices

What is included in this study guide book?

This guide includes one full length practice exams for the OAE Educational Leadership along with detail explanations. The recommendation is to take the exams under exam conditions and a quiet environment.

This page is intentionally left blank.

Practice Test 1

This page is intentionally left blank.

4

Test 1 Exam Answer Sheet

Below is an optional answer sheet to use to document answers.

Question Number	Selected Answer	Question Number	Selected Answer	Question Number	Selected Answer
1		26		51	
2		27		52	
3		28		53	
4		29		54	
5		30		55	
6		31		56	
7		32		57	
8		33		58	
9		34		59	
10		35		60	
11		36		61	
12		37		62	
13		38		63	
14		39		64	
15		40		65	
16		41		66	
17		42		67	
18		43		68	
19		44		69	
20		45		70	
21		46			
22		47			
23		48			
24		49			
25		50			

This page is intentionally left blank.

QUESTION 1

An elementary school principal has a limited budget for the current school year. In particular, the budget will only support one additional teacher for professional development. To effectively use the budget, the principal should support who?

A. a first-year teacher looking to take a training class on instructional methods
B. a librarian seeking to learn the new program implemented to manage the library operations
C. a teacher seeking to take a course to help her add certification to her profile
D. a teacher who is looking to organize a program for afterschool teacher development activities

Answer:

QUESTION 2

A school principal has been informed that there are approximately 150 students without lockers due to availability. The principal will need to make a decision as to what action to take. Which of the following data is less likely needed to make an informed decision?

A. total number of lockers
B. total number of students
C. total number of broken lockers
D. total number of occupied lockers

Answer:

Using the following data to answer the next two questions.

Elementary Education – Grade 6

Summary of Student Performance for Core Subject Areas

- Reading Scores:
    - o 85% of the students are performing below average
    - o 65% of the struggling students are English Language Learners
    - o 5% of the students are performing above average
- Math Scores
    - o 87% of the students are performing below average
    - o 5% of the struggling students are English Language Learners
    - o 7% of the students are performing above average
- Writing Scores
    - o 90% of the students are performing below average
    - o 75% of the struggling students are English Language Learners
    - o 6% of the students are performing above average

QUESTION 3

Which of the following is NOT supported by the data?

A. English Language Learners are doing better in reading than writing.
B. English Language Learners need help in reading and writing.
C. Non-English Language Learners need help mostly in math.
D. All students need help in at least one subject area.

Answer:

QUESTION 4

Which of the following is the greatest need for improvement based on the data?

    A. improvement in writing for nearly all students
    B. improvement in reading for English Language Learners
    C. improvement in grammar for nearly all students
    D. improvement in math for non-English Language Learners

Answer:

QUESTION 5

Which of the following best shows a principal taking a decentralized style of leadership?

    A. not taking formal notes during faculty meetings
    B. allowing teachers to lead faculty meetings
    C. allowing teachers to identify a problem and to plan a solution to implement
    D. allowing teachers to develop their own lesson plans based on the new curriculum released

Answer:

QUESTION 6

Goal of Elementary Education:
Ensuring all students has equitable access to learning curriculum.

The principal is seeking to determine how well this goal is being achieved. Which of the following approaches would be the best to implement?

    A. visiting classrooms while teachers are instructing
    B. analyzing culture background of students who have improved
    C. reviewing disaggregated results from several recent assessments
    D. discussing with students about recent lessons instructed by the teacher

Answer:

QUESTION 7

The principal has noticed a school trend toward declining math scores on statewide assessments. The principal desires to plan professional development activities to address the problem. Which of the following is the best first action to take during the planning process?

A. interview teachers to see what methods are currently being used
B. organize a team of teachers to come up with professional development activities
C. analyze test results to understand specific math skills requiring improvement and subgroups of students requiring additional support
D. analyze test results of previous years with excellent performance on statewide assessments and understand the methods used during instruction at the time

Answer:

QUESTION 8

The Family Educational Rights and Privacy Act of 1974 give parents/guardians of a minor who is getting special needs services the right to

A. remove their child from standardize exams.
B. obtain educational records to share with non-school individuals.
C. select special education services.
D. opt out of IEP meetings.

Answer:

QUESTION 9

A school principal has three teachers who are under emergency licenses as they do not have full teaching certification licenses due to not passing certification exams. The emergency licenses are going to expire in 5 months. The three teachers attempted to take certification exams while under emergency licenses, but all three teachers were unsuccessful. The school principal is aware of their situations and called each teacher to her office to discuss. The school principal informed them that there is an alternative way to continue under emergency licenses by working in a different school in the same district, and the principal expressed support to this idea. The school principal _____

    A. was absolutely correct to provide an alternative approach.
    B. should have put a plan together with the teachers to pass the certification exams.
    C. should have told them that not passing within the next three months will result in termination.
    D. should have informed the teachers that teaching is not the career to pursue if they are struggling this much to pass the exam.

Answer:

QUESTION 10

A new principal has inherited a school with poor performance on all academic measures; this trend has been continuing for several years. The school resides in a low-income community with parents working one to two jobs and long hours. Thus, the parent/guardian and community involvement in school is extremely low. The principal is going to establish a new vision for the school to start moving in the right direction. To get wider stakeholder support and involvement, which of the following is the best strategy for the principal to implement?

    A. communicate the vision to teachers and have teachers spread the vision to the community
    B. provide opportunities for all individuals of the community to participate in different stages of the visioning process
    C. establish the new vision and advertise the vision via website, newsletter, and brochures
    D. communicate the connection of having a school vision to improving in academic areas

Answer:

QUESTION 11

Which of the following is a type of test score that indicates a student's relative position among a group of students in the same grade who are tested at the same time?

    A. raw score
    B. average score
    C. percentile rank
    D. composite score

Answer:

QUESTION 12

The district has communicated to schools the new vision and goal of getting students to use different technological tools to further their own learning. The school principal has recognized that there are not adequate computers, hardware, and software to support students in learning. The principal has reviewed the budget for the current school year, and the principal has discovered there are no funds to support the new vision communicated by the district. Which of the following is the most effective and appropriate way for the principal to use first in the efforts to gain funds?

    A. conducting a fundraiser dinner inviting teachers and parents
    B. asking state representatives for additional state funding
    C. seeking grants that support these types of initiatives
    D. using school credit card to support the initiatives

Answer:

QUESTION 13

All the students were sitting in the cafeteria. A teacher informed one student to do something and walked away. Another teacher then told the same student to do something different. In the cafeteria, the two teachers started arguing with each other. Afterschool, the principal talks to both teachers together. Which of the following is the first action for the principal to take?

A. have one teacher explain what happened and then have the other teacher provide her side
B. start by communicating that this behavior is unacceptable to display in front of students
C. ask the question why they would argue with each other in front of all the students
D. communicate to the teacher the consequences of their action

Answer:

QUESTION 14

A newly appointed school educational leader analyzed the latest state test scores attendance and budget reports. The leader does have some concerns and ideas for possible changes related to thie history department. The leader starts a series of meetings to communicate with the history department. One of the experienced history teachers suggests that the leader may be going too quick with the changes. Which of the following is the principal's first obstacle in moving forward with the changes?

A. creating a new vision
B. overcoming unforeseen district barriers
C. establishing agreement with the new direction
D. creating assessment tools to support the new direction

Answer:

QUESTION 15

A description of the student's current academic achievement level and functional performance is required by:

A. Daily Assessment Records
B. IEP
C. IFSP
D. 504 Plan

Answer:

QUESTION 16

A principal has notice that too many elementary education students at a K-6th grade-level school are bringing cell phones to school. Which of the following is the best and appropriate approach to resolve the problem?

    A. have metal dictators daily when students enter the school
    B. not to return confiscated cell phones back to students or parents
    C. implement a harsher punishment for students who bring cell phones
    D. send a letter to inform parents of cell phone policy and have parents sign the letter

Answer:

QUESTION 17

A principal has notice that certain eighth-grade students, such as ELLs and students with an economically disadvantaged classification, tend to perform much lower than their peers on assignments. Which of the following professional development activity is the best for the teachers to undertake to support struggling students?

    A. establishing assessments that are tailored to struggling students
    B. providing differentiated instruction that builds on students' strength
    C. reviewing instructional methods that have worked with some students
    D. understanding different ways of learning in different countries and cultures

Answer:

QUESTION 18

A school surveys students about their interests in subject areas; the students' responses matter because they are?

    A. relevant
    B. valid
    C. measurable
    D. consistent

Answer:

QUESTION 19

A school is looking to implement a peer mentoring plan to assist experienced teachers to meet district requirements for teacher performance. From a logistical standpoint, which of the following is the greatest challenge?

    A. implement program without increasing the workday
    B. engage teachers to participate in the program
    C. find resources to launch program
    D. pair teachers based on similar educational background

Answer:

QUESTION 20

Prior to the start of the school year, the principal of a middle school assigns 115 students to a seventh-grade teaching team. The team must then divide the students among the five teachers. Which of the following would be the best approach for the teachers to use in making the groups?

    A. using information from students' records to create groups who are likely to function well together
    B. reviewing students' grades and test scores to create groups of students with alike ability levels
    C. giving students the opportunity on the first day of school to self-select the group
    D. randomly assigning every fifth student from an alphabetical list to the same group

Answer:

QUESTION 21

A policy change has been announced by the principal that impacts teachers' ability to provide necessary services to students. The teachers feel that the change will likely reduce their ability to provide necessary services to students. The best action for the principal to take is to

    A. encourage teachers to communicate the pros and cons of the policy to provide a balance view.
    B. encourage teachers to communicate the negative impact the change will likely cause.
    C. start a petition to prevent the change from being implemented.
    D. develop a plan to work around the policy to support the students.

Answer:

QUESTION 22

Strengthening instructional decision making is best done by which with of the following?

A. having access to wide range data on students' assessment for different grade levels
B. having understanding of students' background information
C. having access to updated worksheets and lesson plans
D. having understanding of current standards

Answer:

QUESTION 23

A school last developed a vision 15 years ago. This vision has nearly been forgotten over the years. The new school principal is tasked with initiating the process of developing a new vision for the school. Which of the following indicates the greatest benefit of creating a new vision?

A. provides a purpose for the students and teachers
B. delivers a message of moving forward in a clear direction
C. allows better performance on standardize assessments
D. provides unity between teachers and students

Answer:

QUESTION 24

A newly hired principal has noticed that there is a lack of school's leadership capacity. Which of the following strategies is likely the best in achieving the goal of building school's leadership capacity?

A. provide opportunities to discipline students that normally assistant principals would do
B. provide opportunities to address grade-level and departmental issues by applying collaborative practices
C. provide teachers with training on how to be leaders
D. provide teachers with mentors to develop leadership skills

Answer:

QUESTION 25

A principal is informed by the assistance superintendent that the math staff is weak. What should be the second action by the principal?

A. analyze teacher evaluations to understand competencies of the math teachers
B. review and analyze all students' assessment data
C. have math teachers undergo training courses related to math instruction
D. implement legal strategies for evaluating, disciplining, and dismissing school staff

Answer:

QUESTION 26

Which of the following is the best way to start the process of evaluating teacher quality in a poor-performing school?

A. observe teachers delivering instruction
B. compare students' grade with other schools
C. interview students to understand their learning
D. interview teachers about their instructional methods

Answer:

QUESTION 27

At Blair High School, the principal has received notification that the school must reduce their operating budget by 6 percent for the following school year. Last year, the school was required to reduce the budget by 4 percent. The teachers have expressed concern about their ability to meet goals for school improvement with fewer resources available to them. Which of the following strategies is the best for the principal to implement to address the teachers' concerns?

A. initiate a mentoring program to help teachers resolve new challenges
B. frequently conduct meetings with teachers to understand challenges and possible solutions
C. revise the school improvement plan to aligned with the approved budget
D. challenge teachers to think outside the box for meeting school needs within the budget

Answer:

QUESTION 28

After reviewing the results for state math assessment, the principal notices that one teacher had no student pass the math assessment. The principal reviewed the previous year state math assessment, and the principal notices that no one in the same teacher's classroom passed the assessment. Looking deeper into previous assessment results, the principal notices that majority of the students are performing low on state math assessment from the teacher's classroom. What should the principal do first to resolve the problem?

   A. review qualifications of the teacher
   B. assign a mentor to support the teacher
   C. review past teacher performance evaluations
   D. observe how the teacher is delivering instruction

Answer:

QUESTION 29

An assistant principal, a principal, and grade level teachers are getting together to discuss math scores to improve scores for the following school year. What kind of meeting are they holding?

   A. school improvement planning
   B. grade level planning
   C. teacher development planning
   D. district improvement planning

Answer:

QUESTION 30

Which of the following is the best for a principal to implement to promote various types of culture differences?

   A. have a culture fair
   B. discuss different religions
   C. teach units on different cultures
   D. have parents come talk family traditions

Answer:

QUESTION 31

Which of the following is the best assessment to use to determine whether a teacher is retained for another year?

A. peer assessment
B. formative assessment
C. summative assessment
D. quantitative assessment

Answer:

QUESTION 32

The school counselor has abruptly decided to resign. The position is vacant and will take several weeks or perhaps a month to fill. What is the best action for the principal to take?

A. ask the state to send a temporary school counselor
B. hold off on discussing students' issues until a replacement is found
C. review current staff to see who has the best qualification to temporary provide school counselor support
D. have the school physiologist fill the position of the school counselor

Answer:

QUESTION 33

A principal is approached by a parent who is displeased about instruction relating to world religions that is included in history class. Which of the following described by the parent should be the most concerning to the principal?

A. questioning the existence of God
B. promoting one religion to be more worthy than another
C. having students to learn about practices of different religions
D. allowing students to share information about their own religion

Answer:

QUESTION 34

Which of the following is strictly considered morally unethical?

  A. Principal is taking money from the school operating budget to buy personal items.
  B. Principal using staff time to create worksheets to market online for personal gain.
  C. Principal refusing to provide information to parents regarding his child's grades.
  D. Principal seeking donations for school events from local businesses.

Answer:

QUESTION 35

At a high school, the graduation rate is very high, but the number of students applying to college is 50% of the graduating rate. Which of the following is the best way to increase college admission?

  A. educate the students about opportunities associated with obtaining a college education
  B. give students fee waivers, so they don't have to pay for college application fee
  C. support students in preparation for SAT and ACT exams
  D. provide students with support in applying for colleges

Answer:

QUESTION 36

The clear doors in the hallway are becoming a traffic issue with student transitioning between classes. What is the best action for the principal to take?

  A. replace the glass door with wooden doors with no windows
  B. leave the doors open at all times
  C. remove the doors from the hallway
  D. replace door with shutter proof glass

Answer:

QUESTION 37

Which of the following is the best type of assessment to provide useful feedback for professional development?

A. circular assessment
B. formative assessment
C. summative assessment
D. quantitative assessment

Answer:

QUESTION 38

I. evaluating data to make decision on achieving vision and goals
II. aligning all resources, including technology to achieve the vision
III. outlining criteria to show how instructional programs support the vision

Which of the following are needed to ensure continuous improvement toward the vision and goals of schools?

A. I and II
B. I and III
C. II and III
D. I, II, and III

Answer:

QUESTION 39

The Individuals with Disabilities Education Improvement Act (IDEA)

   A. forces federal government to provide federal funding for early childhood programs.
   B. requires states to create early intervention programs.
   C. requires schools to have funding for improving technology for early childhood special education students.
   D. requires states to provide data to the federal government on student progress in core academic areas.

Answer:

QUESTION 40

In what case does a principal need to evacuate the school?

   A. Bomb threat in the school.
   B. A student brings a gun to school.
   C. Hazardous alert in the community because of a chemical leak.
   D. All of the above

Answer:

QUESTION 41

In decision making process concerning curriculum, the group that is not needed is _____.

   A. curriculum experts
   B. professional staff
   C. boards of education
   D. parents

Answer:

QUESTION 42

A teacher posts something offensive in the teachers' lounge for the first time. Which of the following is the likely consequence?

    A. ban from going into the lounge
    B. termination
    C. letter of reprimand
    D. suspension

Answer:

QUESTION 43

Which of the following is the primary purpose of scaffolding student learning?

    A. ensure students' learning
    B. assist students to become independent learners
    C. encourage positive group engagement
    D. assist students in independently completing assessment

Answer:

QUESTION 44

An open school event is being held at an elementary school. Which of the following is the most effective strategy for showing respect to and sensitivity to the cultural diversity among the families?

    A. have staff to translate for necessary families
    B. have written communication in multiple languages
    C. have staff to support students with disabilities
    D. have student-made posters of different cultures around the school

Answer:

QUESTION 45

A teacher has been working at a school for three months. After evaluating the needs of the district, the teacher has been informed that she will have to go to another school. The teacher refuses this move, and she takes action to abandon the position without in advance notification. The teacher has

    A. been rude to the principal
    B. the right to abandon the position.
    C. taken appropriate action.
    D. breached the contract.

Answer:

QUESTION 46

The school needs to remodel the building. The custodian suggests the construction of one closet for custodians in each floor. Should the principal accept the suggestions from the custodian?

    A. No, remodeling the building needs to take into account the entire school.
    B. No, custodians do not have full perspective of school operations.
    C. Yes, principal needs to take into account all suggestions to make final determination.
    D. Yes, custodians do provide vital services to the school and have some perspective of remodeling the building.

Answer:

QUESTION 47

A student brings a knife to school. Which of the following is the first thing to do?

    A. call the police
    B. contact the parents
    C. see emergency plan
    D. confiscate the knife

Answer:

QUESTION 48

    I.   Are you pregnant?
    II.   Was your military discharge honorable or dishonorable?
    III.   Are you married?

Which of the following are illegal questions to ask during a job interview?

    A. I and II
    B. I and III
    C. II and III
    D. I, II, and III

Answer:

QUESTION 49

A teacher is involved in a professional development growth plan. The best document to show the teacher is what?

    A. support tools available
    B. previous success stories
    C. timeline of activities to accomplish
    D. benefits of completing the growth plan

Answer:

QUESTION 50

Which of the following is the best way to celebrate diversity?

    A. research on Martin Luther King within a lesson
    B. review festivals of Cinco De Mayo
    C. class holiday party
    D. food festival

Answer:

QUESTION 51

The principal invites students to the office to read and share their work; he celebrates teachers too. The main purpose of this is to

    A. show care.
    B. appreciate staff.
    C. promote learning.
    D. ensure learning in school.

Answer:

QUESTION 52

An extra teacher is needed at the fourth and sixth grade level. The principal can only hire one teacher. If the principal can only hire one teacher, at what grade level should the principal place the teacher?

    A. fourth
    B. fifth
    C. sixth
    D. seventh

Answer:

QUESTION 53

Which of the following is the best way for a principal to reduce his or her workload?

    A. add more support staff
    B. delegate responsibilities
    C. work during lunch hour
    D. focus on major issues

Answer:

QUESTION 54

About 25 teachers received middle school certification over 15 years ago. These teachers took certification exams that covered K-8th grade 15 years ago. Currently, certification exams for K-6th grade levels and for 7th-8th grade levels are separate. A new state law is requiring those teachers to go back and take certification for 7th-8th grade in their subject areas. The teachers are utterly disappointed. Teachers are worried about the test fees along with preparation materials. Teachers fear they might lose their job if they don't pass. Some teachers are simply discussing walking out of classrooms to express disappointment with the new requirement. Which of the following is the best for the principal to undertake?

    A. reaffirm the teachers they have the full support of the school
    B. pay for exam fees
    C. provide study materials
    D. challenge the new law

Answer:

QUESTION 55

In the mornings, the school principal has noticed that several buses are arriving late to school periodically. Which of the following is the first step for the principal to take to resolve the problem?

A. conduct a traffic study of bus routes
B. look at the areas the buses are arriving late from
C. talk to the bus drivers to understand the reasons for arriving late
D. have a monitor ride with the buses to understand reasons for arriving late

Answer:

QUESTION 56

In which of the following situations is it most important for a principal to work closely with district's legal advisor?

A. establishing suspension rules for those smoking in school
B. banning suggestive or offensive clothing on school property
C. developing policies regarding visitors coming on school property
D. protocols for establishing consequences for cheating on state exams

Answer:

QUESTION 57

To ensure effective differentiation of instruction in an inclusion classroom, a principal must ensure that teachers must first

A. review students' IEPs.
B. identify the needs of all students.
C. observe students during the first few weeks.
D. have multiple lessons that target different needs.

Answer:

QUESTION 58

What is the maximum number of days a special education student can be suspended?

A. 3 days
B. 5 days
C. 10 days
D. 15 days

Answer:

QUESTION 59

Which of the following is needed to make an informed decision regarding school policy?

A. data
B. support
C. options
D. alternatives

Answer:

Using the following data to answer the next two questions.

Below indicates the budget and expenses for the 2016 school year:

- 2016 Total Budget Available: $70,000
- 2016 Total Number of Students: 670
- 2016 Total Number of Teachers: 40
- Grades: K-6th

Expenses:
- Technology Upgrade: $35,000
- Bathroom Upgrades: $15,000
- 15 Individual Teacher Training Courses: $1500/per course
- Cafeteria Upgrades: $20,000

Total Expense: $92,500

QUESTION 60

The school is overpopulated, and the school needs to upgrade the cafeteria. In addition, the school will need to upgrade some technology to accomplish the district goal of using technology to support learning. The school expenses exceed the budget for 2016. Which of the following modification can reduce the budget and best support the school with the least compromise?

I.   instead of individual courses conduct a group course for training
II. buy only absolute necessary technology to support the district vision
III. defer bathroom upgrades to a later year

A. I only
B. I and II
C. I and III
D. II and III

Answer:

QUESTION 61

Which of the following information is needed to best understand the budget?

    A. The details associated with the training courses.
    B. The details on the increase in square footage for the cafeteria.
    C. The details associated with the technology that will be needed.
    D. The details regarding teachers that might need training in the future.

Answer:

QUESTION 62

A teacher has requested that a student be permanently removed from the classroom. In which circumstances would a principal be most justified in agreeing to the teacher's request?

    A. The student's performance indicates the student will not move to the next grade level.
    B. The student is not doing any assignments and influencing others to not do homework.
    C. The student's behavior is negatively interfering with the teacher's ability to communicate with other students.
    D. The student is barely coming to school and has no interest in learning.

Answer:

QUESTION 63

During the middle of the school year, the air conditioner system in the school is compromised. After an evaluation of the air condition system, the construction contractors indicated that it will take approximately two weeks to repair the damages. Which of the following is the best approach for the principal to take?

    A. buy portable fans and air conditioner units while the repairs are being made
    B. cancel classes until the air condition system is running properly
    C. temporally have the students attend nearby schools
    D. conduct classes outside

Answer:

QUESTION 64

A school principal is very unhappy with a new district policy. The school principal has expressed her concern to the district, but the district stands by the policy. The principal should

    A. ignore the policy.
    B. follow the policy.
    C. get parents to express concern.
    D. continue to contest the policy.

Answer:

QUESTION 65

The principal of a school is reaching out to members of various demographic groups that make up the school community to support in playing an active role in the school. The principal's action best demonstrates

    A. gaining support for success.
    B. getting different ideas to ensure success.
    C. supporting school success by valuing diversity.
    D. ensuring that the community is involved in school decision making process.

Answer:

QUESTION 66

For the school year, the district has adopted new standards, and students are going to be tested on those standards for the upcoming statewide assessments. Towards the end of the school year, more and more parents are opting their child out of the assessment. In this situation, what is the most appropriate action for the principal to undertake?

    A. inform parents that students have been exposed to these standards for some time and the school has prepared the students
    B. inform parents that standards are going to be updated to meet the needs of the future
    C. deny the parents request to opt students out of the assessment
    D. convey the benefits of the assessments to the parents

Answer:

QUESTION 67

Teachers are being evaluated each year on their performance. Evaluation takes into consideration students' performance in class along with district-mandated interim assessments and annual statewide assessments. The teachers are very unhappy as no bonuses or incentives are given with good performance. However, with bad teacher performance, the teachers face consequences. How can the principal best address this issue?

  A. eliminate teacher evaluations
  B. reduce frequency of teacher evaluations
  C. eliminate consequences for poor performing teachers
  D. establish a bonus structure for continuously performing well

Answer:

QUESTION 68

Which of the following is the most important question to answer when using community resources in the classroom?

  A. Are there enough resources to impact the entire school?
  B. Do the resources meet the needs of the school?
  C. Have these resources been used in the past?
  D. What are the limitations of the resources?

Answer:

QUESTION 69

The principal has notice that there are many English Language Learners (ELL) at the school. In reviewing the students' records, most of the students have been classified as ELL for over 5 years. Why is this concerning?

  A. The school does not have assessment tools to determine if ELL learners are ready to go into regular classrooms.
  B. There is nothing concerning about students being classified as ELL for over 5 years.
  C. The school will need more ELL teachers, which might be difficult to recruit.
  D. The students are not being taught effectively to come out of ELL classrooms.

Answer:

QUESTION 70

The school principal has been informed that several staff members are not following district policies on personal and sick time. In particular, the staff has expressed concern that polices are not enforced equally and consistently. Which of the following types of management style is best to implement in developing a plan?

A. directive
B. authoritative
C. democratic
D. affinitive

Answer:

Constructed Response 1

The following table shows statewide assessment data for a high school. Year 3 is the current school year.

Jefferson High School

		Year 1	Year 1	Year 2	Year 2	Year 3	Year 3
Student Group	% of Student Population	% passing reading	% passing math	% passing reading	% passing math	% passing reading	% passing math
All Students	100%	56	42	57	44	63	45
Economically disadvantaged	46%	47	33	49	33	55	32
ELL	30%	33	20	29	27	27	26
Gifted and Talented	5%	5	5	5	5	5	5

As the principal, you have the task of analyzing the data presented in the table. You are to use this information to prepare a memorandum for members of the school district council that summaries the data. In addition, in your memorandum you, need to describe plans for improvement student performance in one or more areas if needed.

The memorandum should include:

- trends of all students and subgroups of students
- analysis of data to support professional development activity tailored to improve instruction in one or more areas of need
- a description of the professional development activity
- a plan to monitor effectiveness of professional development activity

Constructed Response 2

You are in your third year as a principal of a high school. For the last seven years, the school vision has been to focus on STEM subjects and to get students interested in pursuing an education in one of the STEM subject areas. In the initial years of implementing the vision, there was great success in getting students admitted into STEM college programs. Over the years, the rate of students getting admitted to STEM college programs has decreased.

You decided to form a team to develop a focus on getting students to apply to STEM college programs. The team includes teachers, parents/guardians, students, a school counselor, and assistant principal. You will chair meetings of the team.

Examinee Task

Write a memo of about 150–300 words to the team about the plan they will develop. In your memo:

- communicate your views about why it is important for the school to succeed in increasing the number of students to enroll in STEM college programs;
- describe one key factor for the team to consider in developing its plan to increasing the number of students to enroll in STEM college programs;
- identify one type of data or other information that the team should analyze in regard to the specified factor; and
- explain why this type of data or other information would be useful in analyzing the specified factor and meeting the targeted goal.

Constructed Response 3

Use the information below to complete the task that follows.

You are the new principal of an elementary school. The school enrolls nearly 300 students, approximately half of whom are English Language Learners. A review of state assessment for the current year and two previous years indicate that the nearly all English Language Learners are performing below average in reading and writing. The math scores are average and no trends indicate a possible increase in scores.

In a response, you are to :

- discuss one possible approach to support struggling English Language Learners
- identify one type of data or other information that would be particularly helpful in implementing the indicated approach
- explain why this type of data or other information would be useful
- describe one key issue you should consider when initiating planning to implement this approach
- explain the importance of the issue you described in terms of your school's ability to implement the desired change.

Constructed Response 4

Use the information below to complete the task that follows.

Next semester, you will be assuming the role of principal for Bigmenton High School. You currently are employed in another region of the state, so you lack some knowledge of the school and the local community. Before arriving at Bigmenton High School, the central office in your new district provided you some information about the school.

State Test Results for Bigmenton High School

Standardized Testing and Reporting Results for all Students

Three-Year Comparison

The table below displays the percent of students satisfying or exceeding the state standards.

	School			District			State		
Subject	3 Years Ago	2 Years Ago	Last Year	3 Years Ago	2 Years Ago	Last Year	3 Years Ago	2 Years Ago	Last Year
Reading	46	51	53	47	50	52	55	59	59
Writing	44	42	46	46	48	48	52	53	54
Math	31	27	32	36	38	40	44	45	44
Science	43	44	47	44	44	46	43	43	44

Standardized Testing and Reporting Results, by Student Group

Three-Year Comparison

The table below displays the percent of students, by group, satisfying or exceeding the state standards.

Student Group	% of Student Population	Year 1 % passing reading	Year 1 % passing math	Year 2 % passing reading	Year 2 % passing math	Year 3 % passing reading	Year 3 % passing math
Female	52	50	27	55	27	60	32
Male	48	45	33	49	34	49	35
Low Income	60	31	22	30	22	32	26
ELL	15	27	17	28	15	26	18
IEB Students	15	27	16	32	12	29	11
High Income	10	23	16	25	25	26	17

Attendance and Graduation Rates, Last Year

	School	State
Attendance Rate	94%	95%
Gradation Rate	76%	86%

Task

Write an analysis of 500–800 words in which you analyze the data provided. In your analysis:

- identify one critical school issues and/or needs indicated by the data, and explain the significance
- describe two approaches you would use to gain more understanding about the nature or cause(s) of that issue/need and explain why *each* of these approaches would be useful; and
- describe two strategies you and/or your staff should include in a plan to address the identified issue/need, and explain why each strategy you described would be effective.

Test 1 Correct Answer Sheet

Below is an optional answer sheet to use to document answers.

Question Number	Correct Answer	Question Number	Correct Answer	Question Number	Correct Answer
1	B	26	A	51	C
2	D	27	B	52	C
3	D	28	D	53	B
4	A	29	A	54	A
5	C	30	A	55	C
6	C	31	C	56	B
7	C	32	C	57	B
8	B	33	B	58	C
9	B	34	B	59	A
10	B	35	D	60	B
11	C	36	C	61	C
12	C	37	B	62	C
13	A	38	D	63	A
14	C	39	B	64	B
15	B	40	A	65	C
16	D	41	D	66	A
17	B	42	C	67	D
18	A	43	B	68	B
19	A	44	A	69	D
20	A	45	D	70	C
21	B	46	C		
22	A	47	D		
23	B	48	D		
24	B	49	C		
25	C	50	D		

NOTE: Getting approximately 80% of the questions correct increases chances of obtaining passing score on the real exam. This varies from different states and university programs.

This page is intentionally left blank.

Test 1 - Practice Exam Questions and Answers

QUESTION 1

An elementary school principal has a limited budget for the current school year. In particular, the budget will only support one additional teacher for professional development. To effectively use the budget, the principal should support who?

A. a first-year teacher looking to take a training class on instructional methods
B. a librarian seeking to learn the new program implemented to manage the library operations
C. a teacher seeking to take a course to help her add certification to her profile
D. a teacher who is looking to organize a program for afterschool teacher development activities

Answer: B

Explanation: As a new teacher, he or she should have the knowledge on instructional methods. In addition, the teacher can use other coworkers to learn about instructional methods. Option A is incorrect. Option C is incorrect as the teacher is looking to add certification, so the teacher is already certified. This is not an urgent matter to address. Option D sounds good, but option D can result in needing additional funds as the activities are not defined. In addition, most teachers will not want to spend afterschool for teacher development. Option B is the correct answer as the librarian needs to know the program to operate the library.

QUESTION 2

A school principal has been informed that there are approximately 150 students without lockers due to availability. The principal will need to make a decision as to what action to take. Which of the following data is less likely needed to make an informed decision?

    A. total number of lockers
    B. total number of students
    C. total number of broken lockers
    D. total number of occupied lockers

Answer: D

Explanation: The principal will need the total number of lockers and number of students to confirm the problem does exist. As a principal, confirming a serious issue is important. Having the data on the total number of broken lockers will allow the principal to know if the issue is regarding over population of students or simply a locker availability/maintenance issue. Whether students are using the locker is not that relevant as all students will need a locker. Selecting some students to have lockers might result in discriminatory claims.

Using the following data to answer the next two questions.

Elementary Education – Grade 6

Summary of Student Performance for Core Subject Areas

- Reading Scores:
    - o 85% of the students are performing below average
    - o 65% of the struggling students are English Language Learners
    - o 5% of the students are performing above average
- Math Scores
    - o 87% of the students are performing below average
    - o 5% of the struggling students are English Language Learners
    - o 7% of the students are performing above average
- Writing Scores
    - o 90% of the students are performing below average
    - o 75% of the struggling students are English Language Learners
    - o 6% of the students are performing above average

QUESTION 3

Which of the following is NOT supported by the data?

A. English Language Learners are doing better in reading than writing.
B. English Language Learners need help in reading and writing.
C. Non-English Language Learners need help mostly in math.
D. All students need help in at least one subject area.

Answer: D

Explanation: The data provided does not indicate that all students need help in at least one subject areas. In each area, there is a percent of students that are performing above average. It is possible the same student(s) are performing well in reading, writing, and math. All other options are supported by the data provided.

QUESTION 4

Which of the following is the greatest need for improvement based on the data?

    A. improvement in writing for nearly all students
    B. improvement in reading for English Language Learners
    C. improvement in grammar for nearly all students
    D. improvement in math for non-English Language Learners

Answer: A

Explanation: The data shows the sixth-grade class is not doing well in most areas. The greatest area of improvement needed is in writing scores as nearly 90% of the students are below average. Option C does not directly support the data. Option B and C are areas of improvement but not the greatest areas requiring improvement.

QUESTION 5

Which of the following best shows a principal taking a decentralized style of leadership?

    A. not taking formal notes during faculty meetings
    B. allowing teachers to lead faculty meetings
    C. allowing teachers to identify a problem and to plan a solution to implement
    D. allowing teachers to develop their own lesson plans based on the new curriculum released

Answer: C

Explanation: Decentralized style of leadership is when the principal is allowing others to get more involved in identify and solving problems. In other words, the principal is allowing others to take initiative. Having teachers identify a problem and to plan a solution to implement is showing decentralized style of leadership in making decisions.

QUESTION 6

Goal of Elementary Education:
Ensuring all students has equitable access to learning curriculum.

The principal is seeking to determine how well this goal is being achieved. Which of the following approaches would be the best to implement?

A. visiting classrooms while teachers are instructing
B. analyzing culture background of students who have improved
C. reviewing disaggregated results from several recent assessments
D. discussing with students about recent lessons instructed by the teacher

Answer: C

Explanation: The principal will have a better understanding if the goal is being achieved by reviewing data separated into components of recent assessments.

QUESTION 7

The principal has noticed a school trend toward declining math scores on statewide assessments. The principal desires to plan professional development activities to address the problem. Which of the following is the best first action to take during the planning process?

A. interview teachers to see what methods are currently being used
B. organize a team of teachers to come up with professional development activities
C. analyze test results to understand specific math skills requiring improvement and subgroups of students requiring additional support
D. analyze test results of previous years with excellent performance on statewide assessments and understand the methods used during instruction at the time

Answer: C

Explanation: To develop the professional development activities, the principal first needs to understand the specifics of the problem. The best approach is to review the data to see which skills the students (or subgroups of students) need most help with. This will set the foundation to developing effective professional development activities.

QUESTION 8

The Family Educational Rights and Privacy Act of 1974 give parents/guardians of a minor who is getting special needs services the right to

    A. remove their child from standardize exams.
    B. obtain educational records to share with non-school individuals.
    C. select special education services.
    D. opt out of IEP meetings.

Answer: B

Explanation: The Family Educational Rights and Privacy Act of 1974 give parents or guardians of a minor to obtain copies of students' academic records to share with individuals outside of the school system.

QUESTION 9

A school principal has three teachers who are under emergency licenses as they do not have full teaching certification licenses due to not passing certification exams. The emergency licenses are going to expire in 5 months. The three teachers attempted to take certification exams while under emergency licenses, but all three teachers were unsuccessful. The school principal is aware of their situations and called each teacher to her office to discuss. The school principal informed them that there is an alternative way to continue under emergency licenses by working in a different school in the same district, and the principal expressed support to this idea. The school principal _____

    A. was absolutely correct to provide an alternative approach.
    B. should have put a plan together with the teachers to pass the certification exams.
    C. should have told them that not passing within the next three months will result in termination.
    D. should have informed the teachers that teaching is not the career to pursue if they are struggling this much to pass the exam.

Answer: B

Explanation: As a school principal, the goal is to have certified teachers instructing students. So giving the solution that they can work under emergency licenses at a different school in the district is not going to help the teachers reach full certification. The principal should have put a plan together and provided support to pass the certification exams.

th poor performance on all academic measures; this
...rs. The school resides in a low-income community with
...g hours. Thus, the parent/guardian and community
...The principal is going to establish a new vision for the
...tion. To get wider stakeholder support and involvement,
...gy for the principal to implement?

A. communicate ... .chers and have teachers spread the vision to the
community
B. provide opportunities for all individuals of the community to participate in different
stages of the visioning process
C. establish the new vision and advertise the vision via website, newsletter, and brochures
D. communicate the connection of having a school vision to improving in academic areas

Answer: B

Explanation: The question is asking the best strategy to get wider stakeholder support and
involvement. Option A is not going to get all stakeholders involved. Option C does get the
message out to the public, but there is no certainty that the website, newsletter, and brochures are
going to read. Option B gives individual opportunity to participate and express their views,
which ensure wider stakeholder support and involvement.

QUESTION 11

Which of the following is a type of test score that indicates a student's relative position among a
group of students in the same grade who are tested at the same time?

A. raw score
B. average score
C. percentile rank
D. composite score

Answer: C

Explanation: A student's percentile rank indicates the percent of students in a particular group
that received raw scores lower than the raw score of the student. It shows the student's relative
position among a group of students.

QUESTION 12

The district has communicated to schools the new vision and goal of getting students to use different technological tools to further their own learning. The school principal has recognized that there are not adequate computers, hardware, and software to support students in learning. The principal has reviewed the budget for the current school year, and the principal has discovered there are no funds to support the new vision communicated by the district. Which of the following is the most effective and appropriate way for the principal to use first in the efforts to gain funds?

    A. conducting a fundraiser dinner inviting teachers and parents
    B. asking state representatives for additional state funding
    C. seeking grants that support these types of initiatives
    D. using school credit card to support the initiatives

Answer: C

Explanation: Option A is not going to be effective as teachers do not make much money to support these activities. Option B is a good option, but this will take a long time. Option D is not appropriate for the principal to undertake as the funds are not available. Option C is effective and appropriate in trying to get the funds.

QUESTION 13

All the students were sitting in the cafeteria. A teacher informed one student to do something and walked away. Another teacher then told the same student to do something different. In the cafeteria, the two teachers started arguing with each other. Afterschool, the principal talks to both teachers together. Which of the following is the first action for the principal to take?

    A. have one teacher explain what happened and then have the other teacher provide her side
    B. start by communicating that this behavior is unacceptable to display in front of students
    C. ask the question why they would argue with each other in front of all the students
    D. communicate to the teacher the consequences of their action

Answer: A

Explanation: As a principal, getting the information from the source is critical. Giving each teacher the opportunity to provide his or her side of the story establish a foundation of discussion. The other options are actions the principal can take, but the question asks for the first action.

QUESTION 14

A newly appointed school educational leader analyzed the latest state test scores attendance and budget reports. The leader does have some concerns and ideas for possible changes related to thie history department. The leader starts a series of meetings to communicate with the history department. One of the experienced history teachers suggests that the leader may be going too quick with the changes. Which of the following is the principal's first obstacle in moving forward with the changes?

A. creating a new vision
B. overcoming unforeseen district barriers
C. establishing agreement with the new direction
D. creating assessment tools to support the new direction

Answer: C

Explanation: The principal is seeking to make changes in the school. Getting everyone to agree on changes is going to be a challenge. In particular, teachers who have been working for many years will express concerns. The first obstacle the principal will face in moving forward with the changes is establishing an agreement with the new direction.

QUESTION 15

A description of the student's current academic achievement level and functional performance is required by:

A. Daily Assessment Records
B. IEP
C. IFSP
D. 504 Plan

Answer: B

Explanation: Individualized Education Program (IEP) requires a description of the student's current academic achievement level and functional performance.

QUESTION 16

A principal has notice that too many elementary education students at a K-6ᵗʰ grade-level school are bringing cell phones to school. Which of the following is the best and appropriate approach to resolve the problem?

    A. have metal dictators daily when students enter the school
    B. not to return confiscated cell phones back to students or parents
    C. implement a harsher punishment for students who bring cell phones
    D. send a letter to inform parents of cell phone policy and have parents sign the letter

Answer: D

Explanation: The keywords in the question are "best" and "appropriate." For elementary students to have cell phones means those parents are allowing them to have those items. Parents need to be re-informed about the policy to not allow their children come with cell phones to schools. Having the parents sign the letter shows they have read the policy. Option A is a good idea, but it is not appropriate for elementary students.

QUESTION 17

A principal has notice that certain eighth-grade students, such as ELLs and students with an economically disadvantaged classification, tend to perform much lower than their peers on assignments. Which of the following professional development activity is the best for the teachers to undertake to support struggling students?

    A. establishing assessments that are tailored to struggling students
    B. providing differentiated instruction that builds on students' strength
    C. reviewing instructional methods that have worked with some students
    D. understanding different ways of learning in different countries and cultures

Answer: B

Explanation: Students who are ELL or economically disadvantaged have different ways of learning. In fact, all students learn differently. Having the knowledge to differentiate instruction that builds on students' strength will support in providing better instruction, allowing possible improvement on assignments.

QUESTION 18

A school surveys students about their interests in subject areas; the students' responses matter because they are?

    A. relevant
    B. valid
    C. measurable
    D. consistent

Answer: A

Explanation: The students can fill the survey out randomly without any interest, so the responses are not always valid or consistent. There is no indication that the responses are measurable. The students' interest is relevant to learning.

QUESTION 19

A school is looking to implement a peer mentoring plan to assist experienced teachers to meet district requirements for teacher performance. From a logistical standpoint, which of the following is the greatest challenge?

    A. implement program without increasing the workday
    B. engage teachers to participate in the program
    C. find resources to launch program
    D. pair teachers based on similar educational background

Answer: A

Explanation: Individuals will dislike or resist the idea of extending the workday to accommodate mentoring. This will be the greatest challenge.

QUESTION 20

Prior to the start of the school year, the principal of a middle school assigns 115 students to a seventh-grade teaching team. The team must then divide the students among the five teachers. Which of the following would be the best approach for the teachers to use in making the groups?

    A. using information from students' records to create groups who are likely to function well together

    B. reviewing students' grades and test scores to create groups of students with alike ability levels

    C. giving students the opportunity on the first day of school to self-select the group

    D. randomly assigning every fifth student from an alphabetical list to the same group

Answer: A

Explanation: Effective groups are best if the group functions well. Using information about students' records allow the teachers to group students that will work together. This will maximize learning.

QUESTION 21

A policy change has been announced by the principal that impacts teachers' ability to provide necessary services to students. The teachers feel that the change will likely reduce their ability to provide necessary services to students. The best action for the principal to take is to

    A. encourage teachers to communicate the pros and cons of the policy to provide a balance view.

    B. encourage teachers to communicate the negative impact the change will likely cause.

    C. start a petition to prevent the change from being implemented.

    D. develop a plan to work around the policy to support the students.

Answer: B

Explanation: The best option is to be upfront about the change and communicate the negative impact, so the school can reconsider the policy.

QUESTION 22

Strengthening instructional decision making is best done by which with of the following?

A. having access to wide range data on students' assessment for different grade levels
B. having understanding of students' background information
C. having access to updated worksheets and lesson plans
D. having understanding of current standards

Answer: A

Explanation: The keyword in the question is "best." Option A and B seem like possible answers, but Option A is correct as the assessment data will give more knowledge of students' abilities. This is more powerful in instructional decision making than understanding of students' background information.

QUESTION 23

A school last developed a vision 15 years ago. This vision has nearly been forgotten over the years. The new school principal is tasked with initiating the process of developing a new vision for the school. Which of the following indicates the greatest benefit of creating a new vision?

A. provides a purpose for the students and teachers
B. delivers a message of moving forward in a clear direction
C. allows better performance on standardize assessments
D. provides unity between teachers and students

Answer: B

Explanation: The school vision that was developed 15 years ago has been forgotten, so creating a new vision will provide a message of moving forward in clear direction.

QUESTION 24

A newly hired principal has noticed that there is a lack of school's leadership capacity. Which of the following strategies is likely the best in achieving the goal of building school's leadership capacity?

    A. provide opportunities to discipline students that normally assistant principals would do
    B. provide opportunities to address grade-level and departmental issues by applying collaborative practices
    C. provide teachers with training on how to be leaders
    D. provide teachers with mentors to develop leadership skills

Answer: B

Explanation: Option A is not appropriate for teachers to undertake. Option C is not going to allow teachers to apply skills. Option D does not make much sense as the school lacks leadership capabilities. Option B allows the teachers to address real issues using collaborative practices, which can support in teachers' development of essential leadership skills.

QUESTION 25

A principal is informed by the assistance superintendent that the math staff is weak. What should be the second action by the principal?

    A. analyze teacher evaluations to understand competencies of the math teachers
    B. review and analyze all students' assessment data
    C. have math teachers undergo training courses related to math instruction
    D. implement legal strategies for evaluating, disciplining, and dismissing school staff

Answer: C

Explanation: The principal will need to understand the performance of the staff to come up with possible solutions, so Option A is the first step. The question asks for the second action to be taken, which is start engaging in professional development and training. Option B is too time consuming for principal to undertake.

QUESTION 26

Which of the following is the best way to start the process of evaluating teacher quality in a poor-performing school?

A. observe teachers delivering instruction
B. compare students' grade with other schools
C. interview students to understand their learning
D. interview teachers about their instructional methods

Answer: A

Explanation: The keyword in the question is "start." The best first step is to observe to identify specific issues that result in students performing poorly. This approach is the most direct and effective way to start the process of solving the problem.

QUESTION 27

At Blair High School, the principal has received notification that the school must reduce their operating budget by 6 percent for the following school year. Last year, the school was required to reduce the budget by 4 percent. The teachers have expressed concern about their ability to meet goals for school improvement with fewer resources available to them. Which of the following strategies is the best for the principal to implement to address the teachers' concerns?

A. initiate a mentoring program to help teachers resolve new challenges
B. frequently conduct meetings with teachers to understand challenges and possible solutions
C. revise the school improvement plan to aligned with the approved budget
D. challenge teachers to think outside the box for meeting school needs within the budget

Answer: B

Explanation: The teachers are concerned with being able to achieve the school's goals with limited budget. As a principal, the task is to listen to the teachers and seek possible solutions. The best strategy is Option B.

QUESTION 28

After reviewing the results for state math assessment, the principal notices that one teacher had no student pass the math assessment. The principal reviewed the previous year state math assessment, and the principal notices that no one in the same teacher's classroom passed the assessment. Looking deeper into previous assessment results, the principal notices that majority of the students are performing low on state math assessment from the teacher's classroom. What should the principal do first to resolve the problem?

A. review qualifications of the teacher
B. assign a mentor to support the teacher
C. review past teacher performance evaluations
D. observe how the teacher is delivering instruction

Answer: D

Explanation: Data is showing that the students in this teacher's classroom are not performing well. The first step is to see the quality of instruction, which is done by observing the teacher deliver instruction. From there, the principal can recommend some suggestions or actions to improve instruction in the classroom.

QUESTION 29

An assistant principal, a principal, and grade level teachers are getting together to discuss math scores to improve scores for the following school year. What kind of meeting are they holding?

A. school improvement planning
B. grade level planning
C. teacher development planning
D. district improvement planning

Answer: A

Explanation: The assistant principal, a principal, and grade level teachers are looking to improve scores for the next school year, so they are involved in a school improvement planning.

QUESTION 30

Which of the following is the best for a principal to implement to promote various types of culture differences?

A. have a culture fair
B. discuss different religions
C. teach units on different cultures
D. have parents come talk family traditions

Answer: A

Explanation: A culture fair will allow the students to understand the different types of cultures and practices. This will promote the idea of accepting culture differences.

QUESTION 31

Which of the following is the best assessment to use to determine whether a teacher is retained for another year?

A. peer assessment
B. formative assessment
C. summative assessment
D. quantitative assessment

Answer: C

Explanation: Summative assessment is the best to use to determine if a teacher is retained for another year. Summative involves a final or summary judgment of performance.

QUESTION 32

The school counselor has abruptly decided to resign. The position is vacant and will take several weeks or perhaps a month to fill. What is the best action for the principal to take?

   A. ask the state to send a temporary school counselor
   B. hold off on discussing students' issues until a replacement is found
   C. review current staff to see who has the best qualification to temporary provide school counselor support
   D. have the school physiologist fill the position of the school counselor

Answer: C

Explanation: The school counselor is a vital role in the school's organization. The best approach is to assign an individual with acceptable qualification to temporary provide school counselor support. Option A might be a good option, but having someone already in the school staff to support the activities is better as there is a less learning curve of how the school operates. Option B is not the best approach; issues need to be resolved. Option D is not the best approach as the qualifications of school counselor and school physiologist are different.

QUESTION 33

A principal is approached by a parent who is displeased about instruction relating to world religions that is included in history class. Which of the following described by the parent should be the most concerning to the principal?

   A. questioning the existence of God
   B. promoting one religion to be more worthy than another
   C. having students to learn about practices of different religions
   D. allowing students to share information about their own religion

Answer: B

Explanation: The teacher can teach religion in history course; however, the teacher cannot promote one religion to be more worthy than another. Option C is not as concerning as the answer choice states "learn," which is acceptable in history courses.

QUESTION 34

Which of the following is strictly considered morally unethical?

    A. Principal is taking money from the school operating budget to buy personal items.
    B. Principal using staff time to create worksheets to market online for personal gain.
    C. Principal refusing to provide information to parents regarding his child's grades.
    D. Principal seeking donations for school events from local businesses.

Answer: B

Explanation: The keywords in the question are "strictly" and "morally unethical." Option A is considered illegal. Option B is morally unethical as the teacher should not be using staff time for personal gain. Option C is not the best approach for principal to take, but it is not morally unethical. There is nothing morally unethical about seeking donations for school events from local businesses.

QUESTION 35

At a high school, the graduation rate is very high, but the number of students applying to college is 50% of the graduating rate. Which of the following is the best way to increase college admission?

    A. educate the students about opportunities associated with obtaining a college education
    B. give students fee waivers, so they don't have to pay for college application fee
    C. support students in preparation for SAT and ACT exams
    D. provide students with support in applying for colleges

Answer: D

Explanation: The issue is concerning that many students are not applying to college. With a high graduation rate, the students demonstrate the ability to further education. The way to support students is to provide assistance in applying for colleges as the process can be long and confusing to some individuals.

QUESTION 36

The clear doors in the hallway are becoming a traffic issue with student transitioning between classes. What is the best action for the principal to take?

A. replace the glass door with wooden doors with no windows
B. leave the doors open at all times
C. remove the doors from the hallway
D. replace door with shutter proof glass

Answer: C

Explanation: If the door is causing problem with traffic when transitioning between classes, the best approach is not have the doors. Option B seems like a good option, but the students can close the door. The best answer is option C.

QUESTION 37

Which of the following is the best type of assessment to provide useful feedback for professional development?

A. circular assessment
B. formative assessment
C. summative assessment
D. quantitative assessment

Answer: B

Explanation: Formative assessment is ongoing throughout the year for the purpose of improving performance. This is the best way to provide constant feedback for development.

QUESTION 38

I.   evaluating data to make decision on achieving vision and goals
II.   aligning all resources, including technology to achieve the vision
III.   outlining criteria to show how instructional programs support the vision

Which of the following are needed to ensure continuous improvement toward the vision and goals of schools?

A. I and II
B. I and III
C. II and III
D. I, II, and III

Answer: D

Explanation: To ensure continuous improvement toward the vision and goals of schools, principals must evaluate data, align resources, and outline criteria to support the vision and goals.

QUESTION 39

The Individuals with Disabilities Education Improvement Act (IDEA)

A. forces federal government to provide federal funding for early childhood programs.
B. requires states to create early intervention programs.
C. requires schools to have funding for improving technology for early childhood special education students.
D. requires states to provide data to the federal government on student progress in core academic areas.

Answer: B

Explanation: The Act does not force federal government to give funding, require schools to have funding for technology, or require states to provide data. The Act does require states to create early intervention programs.

QUESTION 40

In what case does a principal need to evacuate the school?

A. Bomb threat in the school.
B. A student brings a gun to school.
C. Hazardous alert in the community because of a chemical leak.
D. All of the above

Answer: A

Explanation: If there is bomb threat against a school, the principal is required to evacuate the school. A student bringing a gun to school does not warrant the school to evacuate. When there is a hazardous alert in the community, it is best to stay indoors.

QUESTION 41

In decision making process concerning curriculum, the group that is not needed is _____.

    A. curriculum experts
    B. professional staff
    C. boards of education
    D. parents

Answer: D

Explanation: Recommended practice suggest that parents are not involved in decision making process concerning curriculum.

QUESTION 42

A teacher posts something offensive in the teachers' lounge for the first time. Which of the following is the likely consequence?

    A. ban from going into the lounge
    B. termination
    C. letter of reprimand
    D. suspension

Answer: C

Explanation: This is the first time the teacher has posted something offensive. The likely consequence is letter of reprimand. Termination and suspension are too harsh. Banning from the teachers' lounge is too light of a consequence.

QUESTION 43

Which of the following is the primary purpose of scaffolding student learning?

    A. ensure students' learning
    B. assist students to become independent learners
    C. encourage positive group engagement
    D. assist students in independently completing assessment

Answer: B

Explanation: The purpose of scaffolding is to get students knowledgeable to allow them to independently complete activities.

QUESTION 44

An open school event is being held at an elementary school. Which of the following is the most effective strategy for showing respect to and sensitivity to the cultural diversity among the families?

    A. have staff to translate for necessary families
    B. have written communication in multiple languages
    C. have staff to support students with disabilities
    D. have student-made posters of different cultures around the school

Answer: A

Explanation: Having staff members translate for families with home languages other than English is the most effective strategy. This shows that the school took extra steps to ensure that information is communicated and questions are being asked by all individuals.

QUESTION 45

A teacher has been working at a school for three months. After evaluating the needs of the district, the teacher has been informed that she will have to go to another school. The teacher refuses this move, and she takes action to abandon the position without in advance notification. The teacher has

    A. been rude to the principal
    B. the right to abandon the position.
    C. taken appropriate action.
    D. breached the contract.

Answer: D

Explanation: The contracts of teachers indicate that an advanced notification is required prior to leaving teaching positions. Moreover, common practice is to give an advanced notification, so the school can make arrangements for temporary or permanent replacement.

QUESTION 46

The school needs to remodel the building. The custodian suggests the construction of one closet for custodians in each floor. Should the principal accept the suggestions from the custodian?

    A. No, remodeling the building needs to take into account the entire school.
    B. No, custodians do not have full perspective of school operations.
    C. Yes, principal needs to take into account all suggestions to make final determination.
    D. Yes, custodians do provide vital services to the school and have some perspective of remodeling the building.

Answer: C

Explanation: A good principal will not dismiss suggestions. The principal should accept suggestions from the custodian and evaluate to make final determination of remodeling the building.

QUESTION 47

A student brings a knife to school. Which of the following is the first thing to do?

    A. call the police
    B. contact the parents
    C. see emergency plan
    D. confiscate the knife

Answer: D

Explanation: When information is aware that a student has brought a knife, the first thing to do is confiscate the knife to ensure safety of all students.

QUESTION 48

    I.   Are you pregnant?
    II.   Was your military discharge honorable or dishonorable?
    III.   Are you married?

Which of the following are illegal questions to ask during a job interview?

    A. I and II
    B. I and III
    C. II and III
    D. I, II, and III

Answer: D

Explanation: All three questions are illegal to ask during a job interview.

QUESTION 49

A teacher is involved in a professional development growth plan. The best document to show the teacher is what?

    A. support tools available
    B. previous success stories
    C. timeline of activities to accomplish
    D. benefits of completing the growth plan

Answer: C

Explanation: The teacher is involved in a growth plan, so the teacher will have to accomplish activities. A timeline of activities to accomplish will support the teacher in achieving the growth plan in timely manner.

QUESTION 50

Which of the following is the best way to celebrate diversity?

    A. research on Martin Luther King within a lesson
    B. review festivals of Cinco De Mayo
    C. class holiday party
    D. food festival

Answer: D

Explanation: Option A and B focus on certain groups, so it is not celebrating diversity. Option C is incorrect as some individuals might not participate in holiday parties. A food festival can take into account all cultures and everyone can participate.

QUESTION 51

The principal invites students to the office to read and share their work; he celebrates teachers too. The main purpose of this is to

A. show care.
B. appreciate staff.
C. promote learning.
D. ensure learning in school.

Answer: C

Explanation: Having the students come to the office to read and share their work along with appreciating staff is a way to promote learning. That is the purpose of the principal's invitation. Option B is what the principal is doing not the purpose. Inviting the students to the office is not a way to ensure learning in school; there are much effective ways to do that.

QUESTION 52

An extra teacher is needed at the fourth and sixth grade level. The principal can only hire one teacher. If the principal can only hire one teacher, at what grade level should the principal place the teacher?

A. fourth
B. fifth
C. sixth
D. seventh

Answer: C

Explanation: The best placement is at the sixth grade level. A sixth grade teacher can answer questions associated with fourth grade level. Option B and D are incorrect as there is no need for teachers at the fifth or seventh grade levels.

QUESTION 53

Which of the following is the best way for a principal to reduce his or her workload?

    A. add more support staff
    B. delegate responsibilities
    C. work during lunch hour
    D. focus on major issues

Answer: B

Explanation: In organizations, delegating responsibilities is an approach to decreasing workload. In school organization, this can also promote development of leadership skills. Adding more staff can reduce workload, but there is a cost associated with this approach. Option A is not the best answer.

QUESTION 54

About 25 teachers received middle school certification over 15 years ago. These teachers took certification exams that covered K-8th grade 15 years ago. Currently, certification exams for K-6th grade levels and for 7th-8th grade levels are separate. A new state law is requiring those teachers to go back and take certification for 7th-8th grade in their subject areas. The teachers are utterly disappointed. Teachers are worried about the test fees along with preparation materials. Teachers fear they might lose their job if they don't pass. Some teachers are simply discussing walking out of classrooms to express disappointment with the new requirement. Which of the following is the best for the principal to undertake?

    A. reaffirm the teachers they have the full support of the school
    B. pay for exam fees
    C. provide study materials
    D. challenge the new law

Answer: A

Explanation: This is a big change for the 25 teachers. The principal should not be surprised of the utter disappointment. The best way to establish some calm is to reaffirm the teachers the school supports them 100% in passing the exam. Option B and C are good, but the best approach is to communicate that the school is giving full support to getting the exam passed. Option D seems like a good choice, but the question as for the "best" action. Challenging the law will not do much good in reversing the law.

QUESTION 55

In the mornings, the school principal has noticed that several buses are arriving late to school periodically. Which of the following is the first step for the principal to take to resolve the problem?

    A. conduct a traffic study of bus routes
    B. look at the areas the buses are arriving late from
    C. talk to the bus drivers to understand the reasons for arriving late
    D. have a monitor ride with the buses to understand reasons for arriving late

Answer: C

Explanation: The keyword is "first" step. There has to be reasons for the buses arriving late to school. The principal can talk to the bus drivers to get their reasons. From there, the principal can proceed with additional action to take.

QUESTION 56

In which of the following situations is it most important for a principal to work closely with district's legal advisor?

    A. establishing suspension rules for those smoking in school
    B. banning suggestive or offensive clothing on school property
    C. developing policies regarding visitors coming on school property
    D. protocols for establishing consequences for cheating on state exams

Answer: B

Explanation: A legal counselor advice is required when banning suggestive or offensive clothing on school property as this is an area that can result in controversy in the community. All other options do not require the advice of legal counsel.

QUESTION 57

To ensure effective differentiation of instruction in an inclusion classroom, a principal must ensure that teachers must first

 A. review students' IEPs.
 B. identify the needs of all students.
 C. observe students during the first few weeks.
 D. have multiple lessons that target different needs.

Answer: B

Explanation: Differentiation requires understanding the needs of the students. To ensure effective differentiation, the teacher must first identify needs of the students. Reviewing students' IEPs is a good approach, but that does not take into account students without disabilities. Observing is a good approach, but not the first step for effective differentiation. Having multiple lessons will not be best from a classroom time management standpoint.

QUESTION 58

What is the maximum number of days a special education student can be suspended?

 A. 3 days
 B. 5 days
 C. 10 days
 D. 15 days

Answer: C

Explanation: After 10 school days, under IDEA, students with disabilities must get educational services.

QUESTION 59

Which of the following is needed to make an informed decision regarding school policy?

    A. data
    B. support
    C. options
    D. alternatives

Answer: A

Explanation: The keywords in the question are "informed decision." In order to make decisions, it is critical to have data. Data can be analyzed to know the positives and negatives and allow an informed decision.

Using the following data to answer the next two questions.

Below indicates the budget and expenses for the 2016 school year:

- 2016 Total Budget Available: $70,000
- 2016 Total Number of Students: 670
- 2016 Total Number of Teachers: 40
- Grades: K-6th

Expenses:
- Technology Upgrade: $35,000
- Bathroom Upgrades: $15,000
- 15 Individual Teacher Training Courses: $1500/per course
- Cafeteria Upgrades: $20,000

Total Expense: $92,500

QUESTION 60

The school is overpopulated, and the school needs to upgrade the cafeteria. In addition, the school will need to upgrade some technology to accomplish the district goal of using technology to support learning. The school expenses exceed the budget for 2016. Which of the following modification can reduce the budget and best support the school with the least compromise?

I.   instead of individual courses conduct a group course for training
II.   buy only absolute necessary technology to support the district vision
III.   defer bathroom upgrades to a later year

  A. I only
  B. I and II
  C. I and III
  D. II and III

Answer: B

Explanation: The total cost of the teacher training is $22,500. Doing one group course will cost less, but still result in an over budget. The next step is to buy only technology that is absolutely necessary; there might be room to not buy some technology. There is not enough information to just defer bathroom upgrades to a later year, especially when the cafeteria is overpopulated. Perhaps, there is a critical need for the bathroom upgrades.

QUESTION 61

Which of the following information is needed to best understand the budget?

    A. The details associated with the training courses.
    B. The details on the increase in square footage for the cafeteria.
    C. The details associated with the technology that will be needed.
    D. The details regarding teachers that might need training in the future.

Answer: C

Explanation: The $35,000 for technology upgrade can be for various different aspects and devices. Having details surrounding the technology upgrades can allow exactly what technologies are absolutely needed and critical.

QUESTION 62

A teacher has requested that a student be permanently removed from the classroom. In which circumstances would a principal be most justified in agreeing to the teacher's request?

    A. The student's performance indicates the student will not move to the next grade level.
    B. The student is not doing any assignments and influencing others to not do homework.
    C. The student's behavior is negatively interfering with the teacher's ability to communicate with other students.
    D. The student is barely coming to school and has no interest in learning.

Answer: C

Explanation: The teacher needs to be able to communicate with students effectively to ensure learning. If the student's behavior is negatively interfering with the teacher's ability to communicate with other students, the principal might grant the teacher's request to remove the student from the classroom.

QUESTION 63

During the middle of the school year, the air conditioner system in the school is compromised. After an evaluation of the air condition system, the construction contractors indicated that it will take approximately two weeks to repair the damages. Which of the following is the best approach for the principal to take?

    A. buy portable fans and air conditioner units while the repairs are being made
    B. cancel classes until the air condition system is running properly
    C. temporally have the students attend nearby schools
    D. conduct classes outside

Answer: A

Explanation: Canceling classes for two weeks is not an ideal solution. Sending students to nearby schools can cause additional issues (logistics, transportations, resources). The best approach is to get portable fans and air conditioner units while the repairs are being made; this allows learning to be continued with very little interruptions.

QUESTION 64

A school principal is very unhappy with a new district policy. The school principal has expressed her concern to the district, but the district stands by the policy. The principal should

    A. ignore the policy.
    B. follow the policy.
    C. get parents to express concern.
    D. continue to contest the policy.

Answer: B

Explanation: School principals will not always like the policies that are implemented. Regardless, polices need to be followed. Option B is the best answer.

QUESTION 65

The principal of a school is reaching out to members of various demographic groups that make up the school community to support in playing an active role in the school. The principal's action best demonstrates

A. gaining support for success.
B. getting different ideas to ensure success.
C. supporting school success by valuing diversity.
D. ensuring that the community is involved in school decision making process.

Answer: C

Explanation: The question states "various demographic groups." The principal is valuing diversity to ensure success of the school.

QUESTION 66

For the school year, the district has adopted new standards, and students are going to be tested on those standards for the upcoming statewide assessments. Towards the end of the school year, more and more parents are opting their child out of the assessment. In this situation, what is the most appropriate action for the principal to undertake?

A. inform parents that students have been exposed to these standards for some time and the school has prepared the students
B. inform parents that standards are going to be updated to meet the needs of the future
C. deny the parents request to opt students out of the assessment
D. convey the benefits of the assessments to the parents

Answer: A

Explanation: Informing parents that the students are prepared for the updated standards will give confidence to the parents the students are ready. Option A is the most appropriate to communicate.

QUESTION 67

Teachers are being evaluated each year on their performance. Evaluation takes into consideration students' performance in class along with district-mandated interim assessments and annual statewide assessments. The teachers are very unhappy as no bonuses or incentives are given with good performance. However, with bad teacher performance, the teachers face consequences. How can the principal best address this issue?

    A. eliminate teacher evaluations
    B. reduce frequency of teacher evaluations
    C. eliminate consequences for poor performing teachers
    D. establish a bonus structure for continuously performing well

Answer: D

Explanation: The best way to resolve this problem is to establish a bonus structure for continuously good performance. Good performance needs to be awarded to promote future good performance. Good performance needs to be rewarded especially if poor performance results in negative consequences.

QUESTION 68

Which of the following is the most important question to answer when using community resources in the classroom?

    A. Are there enough resources to impact the entire school?
    B. Do the resources meet the needs of the school?
    C. Have these resources been used in the past?
    D. What are the limitations of the resources?

Answer: B

Explanation: If the resources do not meet the needs of the school, there is no need to pursue in using the resources.

QUESTION 69

The principal has notice that there are many English Language Learners (ELL) at the school. In reviewing the students' records, most of the students have been classified as ELL for over 5 years. Why is this concerning?

    A. The school does not have assessment tools to determine if ELL learners are ready to go into regular classrooms.
    B. There is nothing concerning about students being classified as ELL for over 5 years.
    C. The school will need more ELL teachers, which might be difficult to recruit.
    D. The students are not being taught effectively to come out of ELL classrooms.

Answer: D

Explanation: The goal is to eventually have ELL students enter into regular classroom. For students to be classified as ELL for over 5 years indicates there is something wrong with instructional methods. There is nothing to suggest assessment tools are lacking as the principal is reviewing records.

QUESTION 70

The school principal has been informed that several staff members are not following district policies on personal and sick time. In particular, the staff has expressed concern that polices are not enforced equally and consistently. Which of the following types of management style is best to implement in developing a plan?

    A. directive
    B. authoritative
    C. democratic
    D. affinitive

Answer: C

Explanation: The best way to solve the problem is in a democratic manner, such as having a process of mediation between offending faculty member and a committee of peers. This way the offending faculty member is not automatically considered guilty and has the opportunity to express his or her position. In addition, having a democratic process will address the concern that polices are not enforced equally and consistently.

Constructed Response 1

The following table shows statewide assessment data for a high school. Year 3 is the current school year.

Jefferson High School

Student Group	% of Student Population	Year 1 % passing reading	Year 1 % passing math	Year 2 % passing reading	Year 2 % passing math	Year 3 % passing reading	Year 3 % passing math
All Students	100%	56	42	57	44	63	45
Economically disadvantaged	46%	47	33	49	33	55	32
ELL	30%	33	20	29	27	27	26
Gifted and Talented	5%	5	5	5	5	5	5

As the principal, you have the task of analyzing the data presented in the table. You are to use this information to prepare a memorandum for members of the school district council that summaries the data. In addition, in your memorandum you, need to describe plans for improvement student performance in one or more areas if needed.

The memorandum should include:

- trends of all students and subgroups of students
- analysis of data to support professional development activity tailored to improve instruction in one or more areas of need
- a description of the professional development activity
- a plan to monitor effectiveness of professional development activity

Response: Use email tutoring services to send constructed response to obtain detail feedback and scores.

Constructed Response 2

You are in your third year as a principal of a high school. For the last seven years, the school vision has been to focus on STEM subjects and to get students interested in pursuing an education in one of the STEM subject areas. In the initial years of implementing the vision, there was great success in getting students admitted into STEM college programs. Over the years, the rate of students getting admitted to STEM college programs has decreased.

You decided to form a team to develop a focus on getting students to apply to STEM college programs. The team includes teachers, parents/guardians, students, a school counselor, and assistant principal. You will chair meetings of the team.

Examinee Task

Write a memo of about 150–300 words to the team about the plan they will develop. In your memo:

- communicate your views about why it is important for the school to succeed in increasing the number of students to enroll in STEM college programs;
- describe one key factor for the team to consider in developing its plan to increasing the number of students to enroll in STEM college programs;
- identify one type of data or other information that the team should analyze in regard to the specified factor; and
- explain why this type of data or other information would be useful in analyzing the specified factor and meeting the targeted goal.

Response: Use email tutoring services to send constructed response to obtain detail feedback and scores.

Constructed Response 3

Use the information below to complete the task that follows.

You are the new principal of an elementary school. The school enrolls nearly 300 students, approximately half of whom are English Language Learners. A review of state assessment for the current year and two previous years indicate that the nearly all English Language Learners are performing below average in reading and writing. The math scores are average and no trends indicate a possible increase in scores.

In a response, you are to :

- discuss one possible approach to support struggling English Language Learners
- identify one type of data or other information that would be particularly helpful in implementing the indicated approach
- explain why this type of data or other information would be useful
- describe one key issue you should consider when initiating planning to implement this approach
- explain the importance of the issue you described in terms of your school's ability to implement the desired change.

Response: Use email tutoring services to send constructed response to obtain detail feedback and scores.

Constructed Response 4

Use the information below to complete the task that follows.

Next semester, you will be assuming the role of principal for Bigmenton High School. You currently are employed in another region of the state, so you lack some knowledge of the school and the local community. Before arriving at Bigmenton High School, the central office in your new district provided you some information about the school.

State Test Results for Bigmenton High School

Standardized Testing and Reporting Results for all Students

Three-Year Comparison

The table below displays the percent of students satisfying or exceeding the state standards.

Subject	School			District			State		
	3 Years Ago	2 Years Ago	Last Year	3 Years Ago	2 Years Ago	Last Year	3 Years Ago	2 Years Ago	Last Year
Reading	46	51	53	47	50	52	55	59	59
Writing	44	42	46	46	48	48	52	53	54
Math	31	27	32	36	38	40	44	45	44
Science	43	44	47	44	44	46	43	43	44

Standardized Testing and Reporting Results, by Student Group

Three-Year Comparison

The table below displays the percent of students, by group, satisfying or exceeding the state standards.

		Year 1	Year 1	Year 2	Year 2	Year 3	Year 3
Student Group	% of Student Population	% passing reading	% passing math	% passing reading	% passing math	% passing reading	% passing math
Female	52	50	27	55	27	60	32
Male	48	45	33	49	34	49	35
Low Income	60	31	22	30	22	32	26
ELL	15	27	17	28	15	26	18
IEB Students	15	27	16	32	12	29	11
High Income	10	23	16	25	25	26	17

Attendance and Graduation Rates, Last Year

	School	State
Attendance Rate	94%	95%
Gradation Rate	76%	86%

Task

Write an analysis of 500–800 words in which you analyze the data provided. In your analysis:

- identify one critical school issues and/or needs indicated by the data, and explain the significance
- describe two approaches you would use to gain more understanding about the nature or cause(s) of that issue/need and explain why *each* of these approaches would be useful; and
- describe two strategies you and/or your staff should include in a plan to address the identified issue/need, and explain why each strategy you described would be effective.

Response: Use email tutoring services to send constructed response to obtain detail feedback and scores.

OAE 015 Educational Leadership

By: Preparing Teachers In America™

CPSIA information can be obtained
at www.ICGtesting.com
Printed in the USA
LVOW09s1527130518
577039LV00023B/302/P